GOD'S BREATH OF LIFE

A BOOK OF POEMS

CYNTHIA D. JOHNSON

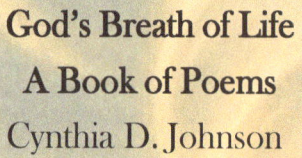

God's Breath of Life

A Book of Poems

Cynthia D. Johnson

Unless otherwise noted, all scriptures were taken
from the King James Version.

Copyright 2025 C.I. No. CI-52116451354
ISBN: 979-8-9985264-8-0
Printed in the U.S.A.

DEDICATION

To the Giver of Breath and Life!

For every moment You've filled my

lungs with purpose,

For every whisper that called me back

to You,

And for the unseen wind that carries

me still.

This book is Yours.

The Breath That Formed Me

Before I moved, before I cried,

Your breath, O Lord, was by my side.

You whispered life into my frame,

And called me forth by holy name.

Morning Wind of Grace

The dawn breaks open with Your

light,

You breathe new mercies into sight.

Your Spirit hovers, soft and still—

My soul awakens to Your will.

The Whisper That Heals

Not thunder loud, not lightning near,

But in Your breath, You draw me

near.

You speak and broken things arise,

You blow the dust from weary eyes.

Revive Me, Lord

Breathe on me, breath of the Divine,

Let dead things rise and broken shine.

Where ashes lay, make beauty spring,

By Your breath, I live and sing.

Living Clay

Formed from earth with heaven's

hand,

I rose because of Your command.

Your breath alone, the sacred spark,

Lit up my soul and warmed my heart.

When I Had No Strength

When I was still and void of light,

You breathed in me Your holy might.

Now I am living, now I see—

Your breath is strength inside of me.

Inhale of Hope

Each breath I take, You first

conceived,

A gift of hope in lungs received.

I inhale peace, exhale the strife,

For in Your breath, I find my life.

Divine Oxygen

The air I breathe is more than air—

It's proof that, Lord, You're always

there.

You fill my lungs, expand my soul,

And speak to me: "I make you whole."

Wind of Purpose

Like rushing wind through ancient

halls,

You blow through me with purpose

calls.

Not just to live, but live for You—

To breathe Your will in all I do.

Silent Revival

Without a word, without a sound,

Your breath came in and peace was

found.

A silent touch, a sacred wave,

That whispered: "Child, rise from the

grave."

Sacred Exhale

You breathe in me, I breathe You

out—

A holy rhythm, dance, and route.

Each sigh, each word, each faithful

song—

Is from the breath You placed so

strong.

The Breath Between My Prayers

Between each prayer and whispered

cry,

You fill the space where I ask why.

Your Spirit flows through every plea—

Your breath becomes my melody.

From Dust to Glory

You breathed and dust became a soul,

With thoughts and dreams and self-

control.

O breath of God, keep breathing still—

Transform my dust to match Your will.

Wind That Walks With Me

Not just above, but deep within,

Your breath commands me not to sin.

You walk with me in breath and

beat—

And guide me with Your grace so

sweet.

Anointed Air

The air around me holds Your grace,

It swirls with love in every place.

It's not just wind—it's proof You care,

Anointed breath is everywhere.

Lifeline

Your breath, my lifeline through the

dark,

A blazing torch, a heaven spark.

When all around me fades away,

You breathe me forward, day by day.

Breath of Belonging

You breathed, and I became Your

own,

No longer lost, no more alone.

Each breath reminds me who I am—

A child of God, not just a man.

Awaken Me Again

When slumber takes my zeal away,

Your breath revives my soul to pray.

Awaken me to purpose true—

Let every breath be filled with You.

Heaven's Airflow

I breathe the breath of heaven's King,

It fills my soul, it makes me sing.

This sacred air, so pure and bright,

Pushes away the shades of night.

Still Breathing God

You're not the God who once just

spoke—

You're still the breath that stirs the

oak.

Still breathing life into the dead,

Still filling hearts and lifting heads.

Breathed Into Being

Before the stars took their heavenly flight,

Before the sun kissed the edges of night,

You hovered gently over the deep—

A breath so sacred, it woke up sleep.

You formed the earth, You shaped the sea,

But then, O Lord, You turned to me.

From dust You crafted form and frame,

And with one breath, I bore Your name.

That breath was power, love, and flame—

It gave my soul a holy claim.

You didn't shout, You didn't roar—

You simply breathed and opened the door.

When the Wind Was You

I felt a breeze upon my face,

So calm, so warm, so full of grace.

It wrapped me tight, yet set me free—

That wind, dear God, was You to me.

When all was still and I was low,

You blew Your Spirit, soft and slow.

Not in the storm, not in the flame,

But in the hush, You called my name.

Your breath restored my broken clay,

It gave me hope, it made a way.

O Breath of God, keep rushing through—

Each time I breathe, I breathe of You.

The Creator's Exhale

The world began not with a bang,

But with the breath from which all sprang.

No hammer fell, no chisel cut—

Just holy breath that filled the gut.

From formless void You made the skies,

With breath You caused the stars to rise.

And when it came to molding me,

You stooped down close—divinely free.

You kissed the clay with breath divine,

And made Your very image mine.

Each breath I draw, a gift, a sign—

That I am Yours, and You are mine.

Breath of My Becoming

There was a time I walked alone,

A lifeless shell, a heart of stone.

But then You came, not loud, not fast—

You breathed on me, and changed my past.

You breathed through trauma, pain, and tears,

You blew away my darkest fears.

Your breath became the lamp I hold—

It warmed my nights and broke my cold.

Now every moment, every day,

I feel Your breath in all I pray.

Your Spirit lives and moves in me—

And by Your breath, I've been set free.

Divine CPR

When I was gasping, faint with doubt,

You leaned in close and breathed me out.

I wasn't strong, I didn't fight—

But You revived me with Your light.

You breathed like fire, not to consume,

But to ignite and make me bloom.

Your CPR—Christ's Precious Reach—

Restored the life no words could teach.

You didn't just sustain my soul—

You made me new, You made me whole.

Now in each breath, I live, I trust—

Revived from ruin, raised from dust.

Wind Through the Wilderness

I wandered dry, a desert land,

No water jar within my hand.

The sun was cruel, the road was wide—

But then, O God, You came beside.

You breathed a wind that cooled my face,

And led me to a resting place.

Not once did You demand a price—

You gave Your breath, Your strength, Your life.

In wilderness, in valley low,

Your breath becomes the stream that flows.

I may not see the path ahead,

But by Your breath, I'm safely led.

He Breathed Through My Silence

There were no words I dared to say,

Just silent cries that lost their way.

But in that hush of aching night,

You breathed, and gave my silence light.

You didn't ask me to explain,

You breathed and lifted all my pain.

A gentle wind, a sacred sigh—

That told my soul: "You're not to die."

Now silence is a holy space

Where I can breathe and find Your face.

You speak in wind, You heal in hush—

And with Your breath, restore what's crushed.

The Breath That Called My Name

Among the crowds, among the noise,

Beyond the reach of earthly toys,

I heard a sound, not loud nor grand—

But like a wind across dry land.

It called my name, it filled my chest—

A breath that summoned me to rest.

No thunderclap, no angel's hymn—

Just breath that broke the chains within.

Now every time I lose my way,

I seek that breath that did not stray.

The one that whispered me awake—

The breath that nothing else could fake.

Breath Over Bones

Like Ezekiel's field so dry and bare,

My soul once gasped for healing air.

But then You came and spoke to me,

"Can these dry bones live and see?"

You breathed, O God, from every side,

And bones arose with holy pride.

What once was death stood tall with might—

Awakened by Your sacred light.

So when I crumble, when I fall,

Your breath revives and makes me whole.

You breathe on bones that men discard—

And crown them kings with beating hearts.

The Breath That Never Leaves

When I awake and when I sleep,

Your breath surrounds me, strong and deep.

I cannot flee it, can't outrun—

The holy air from heaven's lungs.

It followed me through sin and shame,

It didn't stop when others came.

You breathed through fire, storm, and flood—

To cleanse me with redeeming blood.

O Breath of God, forever stay,

Inhale my doubt, exhale Your way.

Each breath I take, each step I move—

Is proof I live because You prove.

Dr. Cynthia D. Johnson

Dr. Cynthia D. Johnson is the creative force behind DSC Publishers, Inc., which has been owned and operated since 2008, began in Central Florida, and is now licensed in Georgia. She has built a team of outsourced vendors over the past 15 years.

She branched out in 2011 to go back to school. After thirty years of graduating High School, she pursued her undergraduate degree in "Early Childhood Development" and a master's in "Human Service

Counseling," focusing on Public Policy & Blended Families. She recently received a Doctoral of Philosophy Degree in Christian ethics & Business Management.

Her company publishes every genre, from children's books to inspirational journals. Her clients mainly consisted of teachers, doctors, and pastors. Erotica books are the exceptions DSC will not publish.

Her educational background affords her, as an author and trainer, the ability to teach book publishing in groups or individual private workshops about the business. Dr. Johnson is a mother of two business-minded daughters, a son-in-law and five grandsons.

CONTACT

If you'd like to reach out with any questions, comments, or to purchase bulk orders and speaking engagements, feel free to contact me at:

support@dscpublishers.com

Social Media

FB @ DSCBookPublishing